Don't Try This at Home

Extreme Jumps

Kay Crabbe

ETA Cuisenaire

Contents

Bungee jumping—
the feeling

Your heart thumps wildly in your chest.
Your lips are dry. You taste the fear.
Your fingers are frozen to the rail, the knuckles white.

Do not look down!

The ground is 160 feet below;
the drop is terrifying.
Shuffle to the platform edge. Hear the countdown:

"5, 4, 3, 2, 1"

"Jump!"

You plummet fifteen storys to the ground, head first.

Panic!

Blood rushes to your head—a sudden surge of **adrenaline**.

You are *dizzy* with excitement and fear.

The ground rushes to meet you.
You are on elastic; the rubber cord stretches to its limit.
It pulls taut. It stops you—just in time.

Awesome!

Boing! You shoot back up.

Up and down, up and down, **rebounding** like a yo-yo.

Finally, you take a breath and... S C R E A M !

Your body pumps with excitement.
You have conquered your fear.
You have bungee jumped!

Vine jumping

How did it begin?

The idea of jumping from a platform with your ankles tied to a cord is not new. The idea came from an ancient **ceremony** that takes place every year on **Pentecost Island** in Vanuatu. Pentecost tribesmen tie their feet to vines and throw themselves from platforms that are ten stories high. This risky **ritual** is called Pentecost land diving.

However, **legend** tells that a woman was the first to vine jump. She ran away from her angry husband and climbed a tree to hide. The woman's husband, Tamale, called her to come down. She refused, so he followed her up. As he climbed, she tied **liana vines** to her ankles. When Tamale lunged to grab her, she jumped out of the tree. Tamale was angry and leapt after her. The jungle vines saved the woman. Tamale fell to his death.

The men of the islands agreed that no one would ever trick them this way again. Every year, Pentecost males cheat death and risk injury to prove their power.

How is it done?

The men build a **framework** of sticks around a tall tree. They weave leaves and branches to make diving platforms in the high tower. Sticks and rocks are cleared from the ground below and villagers stomp on the dirt to make it muddy and soft for impact.

During the rainy season, the liana vines have filled with water and become stretchy, like elastic. The men and boys shred the ends of the vines and tie them to their ankles. The other ends are secured to the tower. Vines are carefully selected by length and age so they will stop a diver's fall just as he tucks his head under and brushes the ground. The islanders believe that a jumper must touch the ground to make the soil fertile, which will ensure a rich harvest of **yams**.

The men and boys stand on the platform, say a few words, and then throw themselves off. If their vines break, or stretch too much, those words could be their last.

Vine jumpers use leaves and branches to build a diving platform.

5

Modern bungee

When was the first jump?

The first we knew of the Pentecost land divers was in 1955 when an article was written by a reporter for *National Geographic* magazine.

Fifteen years later, in 1970, another of the magazine's reporters, Kai Muller, was bold enough to try a vine jump. "I felt oddly unshaken," he said. "Excitement had overridden any physical discomfort."

Stories of vine jumping inspired members of Oxford University's Dangerous Sports Club of Britain to try the stunt. They used **nylon**-braided rubber cords instead of vines. On April Fools Day in 1979, the four "thrillseekers," dressed in top hats and tails, leaped together from the 245-foot-high **Clifton Suspension Bridge** in Bristol. This was the beginning of modern bungee.

the beginning of modern bungee—April 1,1979

How did bungee develop?

When New Zealander A.J. Hackett saw a video of the English jumpers, it fired his imagination. He and a friend set out to develop a safe method of jumping.

They used bridges in New Zealand as test platforms. They measured the height of a bridge to determine the distance of the fall. They worked out the weight of a body and the thickness and breaking strength of cord. They found that factors such as air temperature, humidity, and breeze varied throughout the day. The **elasticity** of the cord also changed after a number of jumps.

After three years of testing, they had a **formula** that worked. No lives were lost in the trials because the bodies were sandbags!

In 1987, A.J. Hackett leaped from the **Eiffel Tower** in Paris. The jump proved to the world that his cord system was safe. He opened his first jump site in New Zealand in 1988.

A.J. Hackett falls through the middle of the Eiffel Tower after his daring leap

the Eiffel Tower in Paris

How is it done?

A **harness** made of bath towels is wrapped around the jumper's ankles and fastened with strong nylon **webbing**. These are called **foot ties**. The jumper wears a waist harness for added safety. Spring-loaded metal-locking clips, called **karabiners,** link the waist and ankle harness to a thick rubber bungee cord.

About the same time as A.J. Hackett opened his New Zealand site, Peter and John Kockleman set up the first commercial site in the United States. They used a multi-cord system. Cords are nylon and are made to **military specifications**. An extra shock cord is added for every fifty pounds of weight.

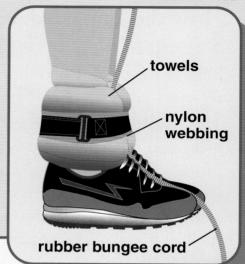

ankle harness

towels

nylon webbing

rubber bungee cord

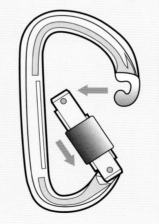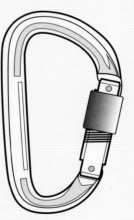

A locking karabiner has a nut that screws over the latch to secure it. Karabiners link the waist and ankle harness to the bungee cord.

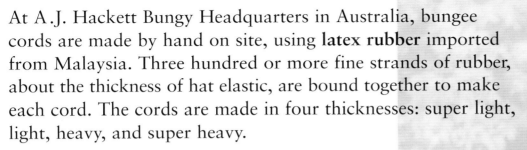

At A.J. Hackett Bungy Headquarters in Australia, bungee cords are made by hand on site, using **latex rubber** imported from Malaysia. Three hundred or more fine strands of rubber, about the thickness of hat elastic, are bound together to make each cord. The cords are made in four thicknesses: super light, light, heavy, and super heavy.

A bungee cord will hold more than 5,000 **pounds,** the weight of a small bus. For safety, a cord is replaced after approximately 600 jumps or exposure to 250 hours of **ultraviolet (UV)** light.

Where else did bungee develop?

Interest in bungee jumping grew quickly. New sites opened in Australia, England, Canada, France, Germany, Norway, and South Africa. Before long, people were bungee jumping from bridges, cranes, towers, hot-air balloons, and helicopters in all parts of the world.

Safe jumps

The crew

Anyone planning to bungee jump must be sure to choose a reliable company.

> "When you are standing on a platform about to step off into fifteen stories of nothing but thin air, trust our jump crew— they know what to do."

These are the words of A.J. Hackett. He says his company conforms to a rigorous code of practice. "Our gear is always individually tested prior to use and constantly monitored during use."

At A.J. Hackett Bungy Headquarters, a 160-foot tower has been built for jumping in the rainforest. Beneath the jump platform, a sixteen-foot pool has been built. Two or more crew operate from the high tower.

Ryan and Rob are Jump Master and Jump Controller. As they climb into their harnesses and attach their safety lines to the tower, Ryan explains their job.

"We constantly check **equipment** with our hands and eyes. We feel the ropes and look for wear and tear," he says as he clips cords together and tugs at **pulleys**.

Ryan moves about the high tower with ease. Just one step behind him is a frightening forty-eight-yard drop, but Ryan pays little attention to it as he unrolls a thick rubber rope and sets up the equipment for the day. "We check the equipment two or three times before a jump," he adds. "Light and heavy cords could be mixed up or foot ties not fastened properly." Checking is crucial—people's lives depend on it.

Ryan shows how the thick rubber bungee cords (approximately 30 feet long) are color-coded and kept separate. Light cords for jumpers weighing under 160 pounds are on the left of the deck, heavier cords on the right. "We can add two or more cords together and build a big bungee rope for heavy weights," he says.

The cords are color-coded to match the weights they can support: **black**—super heavy, **green**—super light, **blue**—heavy, **red**—light.

The customers

Rob checks Ryan's moves as he prepares Denise for her first jump. She steps into a waist harness with leg loops, the type used by rock climbers. She sits on a large box, legs out in front. She is nervous.

Ryan makes a bandage of bath towels and wraps it around Denise's ankles. He binds the towels tightly with a length of nylon webbing. Its end strap is pulled between her ankles. A wider tape is wound over the top to ensure that Denise's foot ties stay in place.

Ryan connects a karabiner from the foot strap to the thick rubber bungee cord. The cord has a short static safety line attached. This is locked onto Denise's waist harness. A static cord does not stretch much; it is used to lower a jumper into the raft after their jump.

Music thumps through the loudspeakers as Denise shuffles to the edge of the small platform. The sun is shining and the view over the tops of trees and out to sea is spectacular. In the distance, Green Island juts out of the waters of the **Great Barrier Reef**.

But Denise looks down—it is fifteen stories to the bottom. Her face turns a ghostly white. Her knees tremble with fear. She shuffles back. She cannot summon the courage to do it.

Ryan and Rob watch Denise closely. They speak softly, reassuring her that every safety precaution has been taken. "Trust us," Ryan says. "Safe bungee is our business."

Luke sits and waits in an **inflatable raft** on the pool below. It is his job to paddle out and bring the jumper in. When a bungee jump is complete, the person is left suspended in the air, dangling head first over the pool on a rubber cord. Luke hooks the short static cord with his paddle and eases the jumper into the raft. He unhooks the karabiners, undoes the harnesses, and paddles the ten or fifteen feet back to land.

Denise shuffles along the high platform a second time. Her toes grip the edge. "Look straight ahead," Ryan whispers. But Denise looks down. She is scared stiff. There's a long pause.

"I can't do it," Denise cries. She backs off.

Axel, a young man from Germany, is keen to jump and does not need coaching. "I'm scared," he confesses, "but I want to get over my fear." He climbs into his harness, smiles for the camera, and shouts, "Let's do it!"

A loud **"Yahoo!"** fills the air as Axel dives head first to the bottom. The bungee cord stretches to its limit. His head skims the surface of the water. There is a quick splash, then he flies back up again.

Steve paces as he waits. "I hate heights. They scare me," he admits, as he looks down over the railing. "But I want a job as a fireman; I'll have to climb high ladders." His face turns a sickly shade of gray and he steps away. "Jumping will cure my fear—I hope." Steve fiddles with his ticket. He has paid for an unlimited number of jumps. He will be back.

Denise sits and watches. She is still wearing her waist harness. "Do you want to try again?" Ryan asks.

"I'm thinking about it," she answers.

More daring jumps

Riskier jumps

At A.J. Hackett Bungy Headquarters, children must be over thirteen years of age to jump. The oldest man to bungee jump from the tower was eighty-three, the oldest woman seventy-six.

People jump two at a time. They jump on skateboards and mountain bikes, in shopping trolleys and **kayaks**. Once, six people jumped in a rubber raft!

Higher jumps

Bungee jumpers have also gone to great heights to add more distance to their **free fall**. A.J. Hackett leaped 148 yards from a **cable car** in New Zealand and 328 yards from a helicopter. He jumped from the world's highest suspension bridge, the 362-yard Royal Gorge Bridge in Colorado. It has been reported that others have bungee jumped 499 yards, the height of a 150-story skyscraper.

a close-up photograph of a worn bungee cord

Accidents

Most bungee accidents are caused by human error or on unsafe sites. People have been injured when safety equipment has not been properly attached, when cords of the wrong length are used, or when worn cords are not replaced.

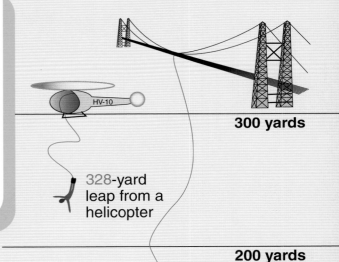

some of A.J. Hackett's biggest and most dangerous jumps

300 yards

328-yard leap from a helicopter

200 yards

362-yard leap from Royal Gorge Bridge, Colorado

100 yards

148-yard leap from a cable car

Ground level

Sky jumps

The early parachute jumps

The world's first successful **parachute** jump was in 1783, when Sebastian Lenormand floated from a tower to the ground. In 1797, André Jacques Garnerin made the first successful parachute jump from a hot-air balloon over Paris.

Sky diving today

Today, a person can jump out of a plane, pull a **rip cord**, and glide around the sky on a small, wing-shaped **canopy**. Beginners are taught to open their chute once they are clear of the aircraft, but more experienced sky divers like to free fall.

In spectacular displays, sky divers free fall together, then join up, and hold on to one another to form patterns in the sky. The current largest free-fall formation record was set in December 1999. Two hundred eighty-two sky divers came together for 7.11 seconds in the skies over Thailand.

Sky divers wear a harness and a backpack. A container is attached which stores a main canopy and a second one—a reserve. This is used if the main parachute malfunctions.

Most sky divers carry an **automatic activation device (AAD)** for an emergency. Its computer senses when a pre-set altitude is passed at high speed, and the reserve canopy opens.

Ram-air canopies are used for sky diving. They are easier to steer than the round umbrella parachutes and give a softer, more exact landing.

In stack canopy formation, jumpers open their chutes and link up, stacking one above the other. Each jumper hooks his legs into the lines of the canopy below.

Sky surfers

In the 1980s, keen sky divers who wanted to do more than turns and twists and free-fall formations began to experiment on surfboards. This led to a new **extreme** sport called sky surfing.

Joel Cruciani, a French sky diver, was the first to free fall with a surfboard strapped to his feet. He performed the stunt in 1987 for the film, *Hibernator*.

Sky boards today are small and lightweight. They have foot bindings that allow a sky surfer to release the board in an emergency or just before landing.

Foot bindings allow a sky surfer to release the board before landing.

In competitions, expert sky surfers jump with a second person, a **camera-flier**, who wears a helmet with a built-in video camera. As the two flip, roll, and spin together, the camera-flier videos the sky surfer's stunts.

Camera-fliers wear suits with panels called wings that go from their wrists to their waist or hips. As they lift their arms, the wings open out and fill with air to slow their speed. The wings collapse gradually as the flier tucks their arms back in.

Sky surfing is a dangerous sport. If a spin goes out of control, the surfer could become confused or even unconscious in the air. Canopies could tangle or fail to open. Surfers must stay alert and concentrate.

The first Sky Surfing World Championships were held in Spain in 1993. In 1994, sky surfing was included in the opening ceremony of the Winter Olympics at Lillehammer, Norway.

Glossary

adrenaline   hormone released by a gland in the body; speeds up heartbeat and raises energy levels

automatic activation device (AAD)   device that opens a reserve parachute

cable car   carriage pulled by a moving cable; ski lift

camera-flier   sky diver who wears a video camera

canopy   *see* parachute

ceremony   act performed on special occasion

Clifton Suspension Bridge   bridge in Bristol, England; site of the first modern bungee jump

Eiffel Tower   a famous iron tower in Paris over 300-feet high

elasticity   stretch

equipment   tools, gear

extreme   of the highest level

foot tie   ankle bandage

formula   method or rule

framework   support structure

free fall   fall sharply with no restraint

Great Barrier Reef   world's longest coral reef— in Queensland, Australia

harness   bands and straps worn for safety

inflatable raft   rubber boat filled with air

karabiner   metal locking clip

kayak   light canoe

latex rubber   elastic material made from natural rubber

legend   story handed down through the ages

liana vine   tropical climbing plant

military specifications   army rules

nylon   strong elastic material

parachute   umbrella-shaped device used to descend safely
  through the air

Pentecost Island   part of Vanuatu; place where vine
  jumping began

pulley   grooved wheel for a rope to run on

rebound   spring back

rip cord   cord or ring pulled to open parachute

ritual   act preformed in a ceremony

suspension bridge   road hung on cables between towers

ultraviolet (UV)   invisible rays from the sun

webbing   strong, tightly woven strip of cloth

yam   root vegetable (sweet potato)

Index